HANDS-ON GEOLOGY

Get Hands-On with Tectonic Plates!

Alix Wood

Full of real geology experiments to help learn about Earth's tectonic plates.

PowerKiDS press

New York

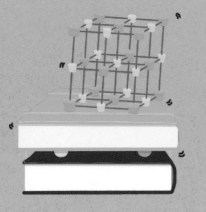

Published in 2022 by Rosen Publishing
29 East 21st Street, New York, NY 10010

Produced for Rosen Publishing by Alix Wood Books
Designed by Alix Wood
Editor: Eloise Macgregor
Consultant: Kate Spencer, Professor of Environmental Geochemistry

Cataloging-in-Publication Data
Names: Wood, Alix.
Title: Get hands-on with tectonic plates! / Alix Wood.
Description: New York : PowerKids Press, 2022. | Series: Hands-on geology |
Includes glossary and index.
Identifiers: ISBN 9781725331310 (pbk.) | ISBN 9781725331334 (library bound) |
ISBN 9781725331327 (6 pack) | ISBN 9781725331341 (ebook)
Subjects: LCSH: Plate tectonics--Juvenile literature.
Classification: LCC QE511.4 W66 2022 | DDC 551.1'36--dc23

Photo credits:
4 , 6, 7 top left, 8, 9 top, 12, 14 and 15 top, 16, 20 middle, 21 top, 22 and 23
background, 22 insets, 24, 26 middle right and bottom, 28, 29 top © AdobeStock
Images; 5 bottom public domain; 10 NOAA/public domain; 13 top public domain; 15
middle John Wiley/public domain; all other illustrations @ Alix Wood

Printed in the United States of America

CPSIA Compliance Information: Batch #CSPK22. For Further Information contact Rosen Publishing, New York, New York at 1-800-237-9932.

Contents

What Are Tectonic Plates?

Earth is made up of many layers. We live on the thin outer layer, known as Earth's **crust**. Although the crust seems stable, it is actually constantly moving. The large rock slabs under our feet rest on a hot, semiliquid layer below the crust called the **mantle**. These huge slabs are known as tectonic plates. Tectonic plates run under both the land and the oceans. They connect together a little like a giant jigsaw.

crust

mantle

outer core

inner core

Earth's Tectonic Plates

Juan de Fuca

North American

Eurasian

Pacific

Caribbean

Cocos

Pacific

Nazca

South American

African

Arabian

Indian

Philippines

tectonic plate boundaries

Australian

Antarctic

Scotia

Think About This...

?

Why do you think rock in the mantle nearest to Earth's crust is firmer than rock closer to Earth's outer core?

The temperature gets hotter and the pressure gets higher toward the center of Earth. The weight of the surrounding Earth presses the **dense**, hot, melted metals into a solid ball at the **core**. Hot liquid rock and semiliquid rock around the core forms the mantle. The mantle closest to the crust is cooler and firmer.

HANDS-ON   Is Earth Like an Egg?

You will need:
- a blunt or plastic knife
- a hard-boiled egg
- some markers

The inside of Earth is a little like an egg, with its thin crusty shell and semisolid middle layer.

Draw some oceans and **continents** on your egg shell using the markers. Then gently tap the hard-boiled egg on a table. This should produce cracks in the shell, a little like the cracks separating Earth's tectonic plates.

Peel off the shell of the egg. The shell is like Earth's crust, a quite thin layer of crusty rock. The next layer you can see is the white of the egg, which is a little like the mantle of Earth. Like the mantle, it is not completely solid.

Cut your egg in half and you will see the yolk, which represents Earth's core. The core would really be a hard solid ball though, not soft like an egg yolk.

How Do We Know Tectonic Plates Move?

We can't feel the ground under our feet moving. How do we know it does? In 1912, German scientist Alfred Wegener studied the shapes of the west coast of Africa and eastern South America. They looked like they could fit together like a jigsaw. He thought the continents must have once been joined together.

Alfred Wegener

Africa

South America

He then discovered matching **fossils** of plants and animals had been found in both Africa and South America. The fossils were of animals that could not have traveled across oceans. Evidence of icy glaciers in hot countries such as India and Africa also made him think Earth's crust must move.

5

An Ever-Changing Earth

Earth's tectonic plates have been moving across its surface for hundreds of millions of years. As the plates move, the continents on them move, too. Scientists think that a number of enormous "supercontinents" have formed and broken apart over Earth's history. This happens very slowly, though. They believe it takes around 500 million years for all the continents to join together into one big continent, and then break apart again.

Pangaea

The most recent supercontinent was Pangaea. It formed around 270 million years ago. As it lay across a tectonic plate **boundary**, it slowly broke apart. Hot melted rock known as **magma** rose and filled the space and became the floor of the Atlantic Ocean.

An area of Pangaea containing North America, Europe, and Asia gradually drifted north. The piece with Antarctica, Africa, South America, and Australia drifted south. Then these continents broke apart and slowly moved to where they are now.

HANDS-ON
Puzzle Pieces

Look at the map of Pangaea above, and compare it to a globe or world map. Can you see the outlines of any modern continents within Pangaea?

In around 250 million years, some geologists believe the continents will have all joined together again!

BE A GEOLOGIST
Make Your Own Supercontinent

You Will Need:

- tracing paper
- a pencil
- masking tape
- scissors

The Geology:

Geologists have different opinions about whether **landmasses** are getting bigger, smaller, or staying the same, but they all agree that Earth's crust is moving and changing. Scientists are not sure what shape the next supercontinent will be. What do you think?

How to Make a Supercontinent:

The simplified map below shows the largest areas of land on the globe. Cutting around every island would be very hard! If you want to try, use a more detailed map. Place the tracing paper on the map and hold it steady using some masking tape. Trace around each landmass using a pencil. Cut each landmass out. Because tectonic plates cross some of the continents, you should separate North America from South America, separate Africa from Europe, and separate India from Asia along the red dotted line. Can you assemble your land to make a new supercontinent? Which areas fit together best? How many oceans do you have?

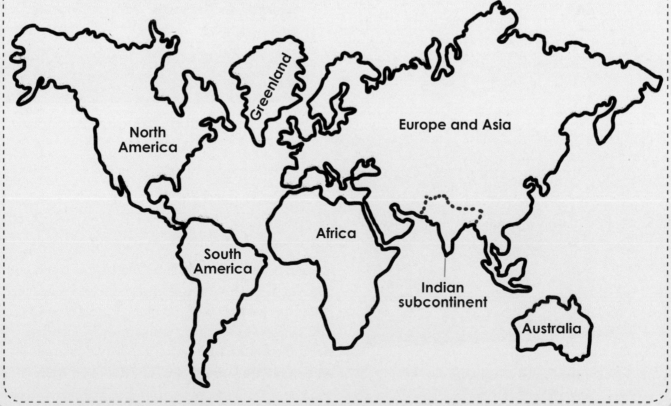

How Does the Earth Move?

Earth is split into seven major plates and eight smaller plates. Along each boundary the plates can move against each other in three possible ways. They can push against one another, move away from each other, or slide past one another.

Convergent boundaries

When two plates push against each other, it is known as a convergent boundary. The **collision** can buckle the earth and form mountain ranges. The Himalayan Mountains formed when the Indian Plate collided with the Eurasian Plate. **Volcanoes** are often found along convergent boundaries.

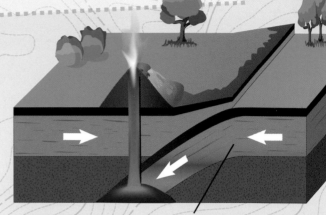

Sometimes (usually when ocean and land plates meet) the denser plate will move under the other plate at a convergent boundary.

Divergent boundaries

Divergent plate boundaries slide apart. Magma seeps up through the gap, then cools and turns to rock, making new crust on the edge of the plates. Lava eruptions and **geysers** occur along these rifts.

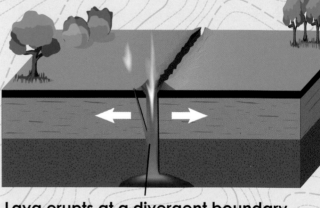

Lava erupts at a divergent boundary.

A rift forming at a divergent boundary in Iceland.

Think About This... ?

Iceland is on a divergent boundary between the North American and Eurasian Plates. Eastern Iceland is moving east with the Eurasian Plate, and the western part is moving west with the North American Plate. Do you think Iceland will split into two landmasses, or become larger?

Transform boundaries

At a transform plate boundary, two plates grind past each other. These plate boundaries do not allow magma to seep upward, so there is no new crust being created or broken down. These spots are often the site of **earthquakes**.

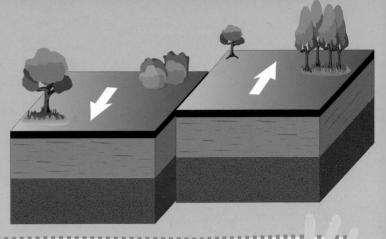

HANDS-ON Try Moving Boundaries

You will need:
- several crackers
- some frosting
- a plate

Cover a plate with frosting. The frosting represents Earth's mantle. Place two crackers on the frosting. The crackers are tectonic plates. Now experiment moving your plates in the three ways that plates move against one another.

BE A GEOLOGIST
Explore How Continents Move

You Will Need:
- a large baking sheet
- shaving foam or frosting
- card stock
- scissors

How to Do the Experiment:

Cover a baking tray in shaving foam or frosting. Roughly draw the plates in the map below onto card stock. Draw on the direction arrows. Cut out the plates. Place the plates on the foam and try to move each plate in the direction of its arrows. Can you see how each movement affects the plates that surround it?

The Geology:

The way one plate boundary moves affects how that plate moves against other plates. Earth is a little like a huge sliding puzzle!

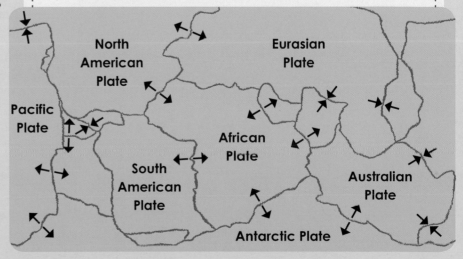

Oceanic Spreading

Earth's crust is thinner, younger, and denser under the oceans. A giant system of undersea **ridges** create new rock. When two plates of oceanic crust move apart, **molten lava** flows up through the gap, creating new crust. Older oceanic crust is pushed outward and sinks down **trenches** into the mantle. Because they are constantly creating new crust in these areas, the ocean is slowly spreading, pushing the tectonic plates apart.

Iceland

Mid-Atlantic Ridge

The Mid-Atlantic Ridge (MAR) is a huge ridge on the floor of the Atlantic Ocean. Its divergent boundary is slowly sliding apart. Although mostly underwater, some of the ridge is visible in Iceland. The ridge sits on the Mid-Atlantic Rise, a bulge running through the Atlantic Ocean. The bulge is believed to have been caused by hot **currents** pushing up the oceanic crust.

The Atlantic Ocean is getting bigger, creating new rock faster than older rock can sink back down. It is growing about one inch (2.5 cm) per year. The Pacific Ocean is getting smaller. Its older crust is sinking into the deep Mariana Trench faster than it can create new rock.

Think About This... ❓

What is the longest mountain range on Earth? The Mid-Atlantic Ridge is part of the enormous Mid-Ocean Ridge. The ridge wraps right around Earth but is 90 percent underwater!

HANDS-ON Make a Ridge Simulator

You will need:
- paper
- colored pencils
- scissors
- a tissue box

Color some wide stripes across your paper. Cut the paper in half lengthwise so you have two matching strips. Feed the strips into the slit of a tissue box. You may have to cut them to fit.

The slit is your Mid-Ocean Ridge. Pull both strips slowly out of the slit and over each side of the box. The stripes that appear on the strips are the new rock forming from the ridge and then sinking down at the sides of the box.

BE A GEOLOGIST
See How Oceanic Trenches Work

You Will Need:

- some card stock
- markers
- scissors
- a baking sheet
- frosting or shaving foam
- a spoon

How To Do The Experiment:

Cut a piece of card stock so it is just slightly smaller than your baking sheet. Roughly cut the card stock into four strips lengthwise. Color two pieces to look like land and two pieces to look like ocean floor.

Put a layer of frosting or shaving foam on your baking sheet. Place the land pieces at the side edges of the sheet. Rest the ocean floor pieces in the middle. Start to slide the two ocean pieces apart using a spoon. When the ocean floor starts to touch the land, gently press down on the ocean edges so the plates run under the land. Then you can continue to push your ocean floor apart at the ridge.

The Geology:

When a tectonic plate is forced down underneath another plate, it's known as **subduction**. This is how old rock sinks back down into Earth's hot mantle and gets recycled.

Sinking Plates

Scientists used to believe that currents in the mantle caused by heat from Earth's core caused it to slowly move the crust around. Geologists now also think that plates move by a process known as slab pull. When older, denser tectonic plates sink into the mantle, the newer, less dense sections get pulled along behind them. This sinking in one place leads to the plates spreading apart in another place.

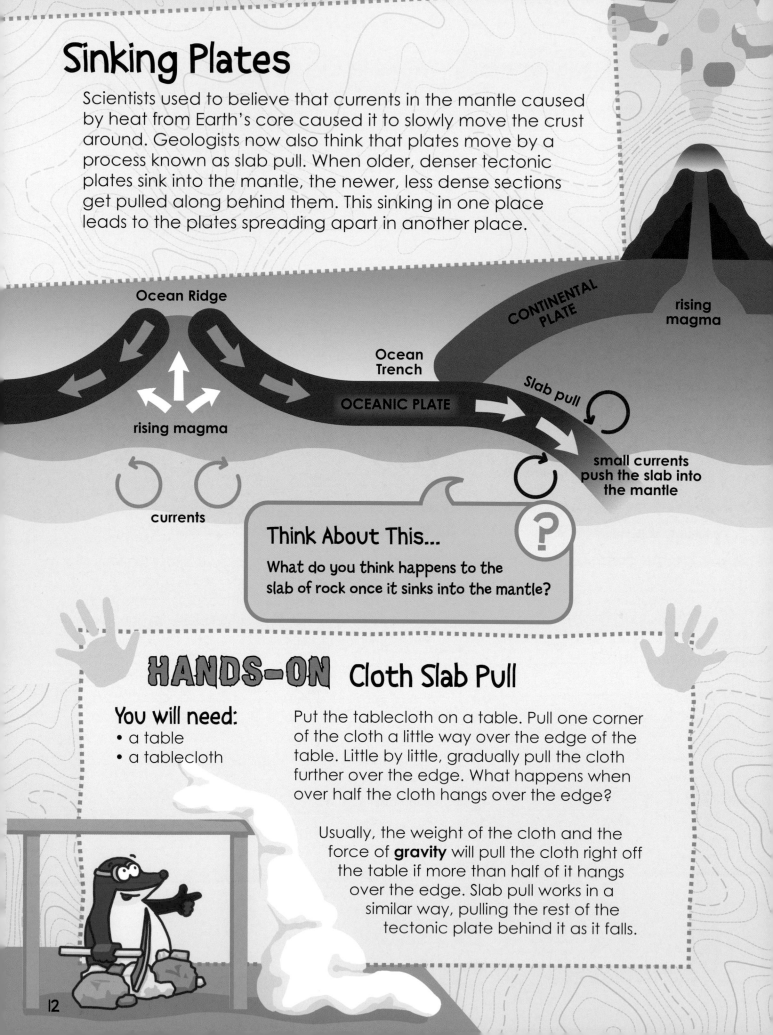

Ocean Ridge

CONTINENTAL PLATE

rising magma

Ocean Trench

OCEANIC PLATE

Slab pull

rising magma

small currents push the slab into the mantle

currents

Think About This...

What do you think happens to the slab of rock once it sinks into the mantle?

HANDS-ON Cloth Slab Pull

You will need:
- a table
- a tablecloth

Put the tablecloth on a table. Pull one corner of the cloth a little way over the edge of the table. Little by little, gradually pull the cloth further over the edge. What happens when over half the cloth hangs over the edge?

Usually, the weight of the cloth and the force of **gravity** will pull the cloth right off the table if more than half of it hangs over the edge. Slab pull works in a similar way, pulling the rest of the tectonic plate behind it as it falls.

Deep Ocean Trenches

When a **continental plate** meets an **oceanic plate**, the denser oceanic plate drops under the lighter continental plate, forming a trench. Two oceanic plates can also form trenches. The Pacific Plate is falling beneath the smaller Mariana Plate, forming the Mariana Trench. The Pacific Plate subducts because its rock is older, denser, and colder.

The Mariana Trench, at 6.82 miles (10.97 km) deep, is the deepest known place on Earth, but oddly, it is not the part of the ocean floor closest to Earth's core. Why? Because Earth is not a perfect sphere.

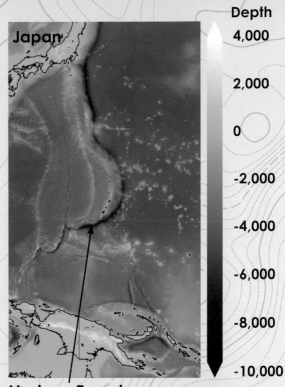

Japan

Depth
4,000
2,000
0
-2,000
-4,000
-6,000
-8,000
-10,000
meters

Mariana Trench

BE A GEOLOGIST
Bathymetry - Map the Ocean Floor

You Will Need:

- a shoebox with lid
- modeling clay
- a wooden skewer
- squared paper
- colored markers
- tape

The Geology:

Bathymetry is the measurement of depth of water. Geologists measure the depth of the seafloor using **sonar**. They measure the time it takes for sound waves to travel from the ship to the seafloor and back.

How to Do the Experiment:

Mold a seafloor in the bottom of a shoebox using modeling clay. Include mountains and trenches. Let the clay harden. Tape the squared paper to the lid. Poke a hole in each square. Label each axis with numbers and letters.

Mark the wooden skewer every half inch or centimeter with a different color. Poke the skewer through each grid hole until it touches the seafloor. Record the depth on your grid by shading the square in the correct color.

World-Shaking Earthquakes

Earthquakes happen along plate boundaries. When two plate boundaries move against each other, the rock can stick and then suddenly break away again with great force. This can cause an earthquake. The released energy moves through Earth in the form of waves, which shake the ground. The place where Earth's crust snaps is called a **fault**.

BE A GEOLOGIST
Understanding Stored Energy

You Will Need:

- cheese slices
- a blunt knife
- some candy

The Geology:

Just like your cheese slice, the edges of tectonic plates are rough. They can get stuck to each other while the rest of the two plates keep moving. When the edges suddenly give way, the released stored energy causes the plates to shake.

How to Do the Experiment:

To make two tectonic plates, cut a stack of cheese slices down the middle. Cut another slice in a zigzag down the middle. Place a zigzag half on each stack, zigzag sides together. Balance some pieces of candy on top of the slices.

Slowly slide the two plates away from each other. You should feel the bottom move easily, but the zigzag crust will stick a little. When the top layer breaks free, the released stored energy should shake the candy.

Think About This...

If two plates' edges are smooth and don't stick together, do we feel them move?

HANDS-ON Make a Shake Table

You will need:
- two large books
- four bouncy balls or marbles
- two large rubber bands

Try earthquake experiments using this simple shake table. Place the balls between two books. Wrap the rubber bands around the books to hold them and the balls in place.

If you wobble the top book it will behave a little like a real earthquake. Use your shake table for the experiment on page 19.

The San Andreas Fault

The San Andreas Fault (right) in California is a transform fault where the Pacific and North American Plates meet. The Pacific Plate slides northwest and the North American Plate slides south east. The fault is around 800 miles (1,287 km) long and ten miles (16 km) deep—and is still growing. Many earthquakes occur along this fault.

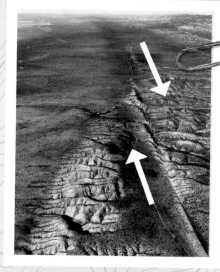

Earthquake Facts

- Hundreds of earthquakes happen every day, but they are either too small, too far below the surface, or deep in the oceans for us to feel them.

- Earthquakes can be felt over large areas. In 1985, an earthquake in Mexico caused water to slosh from a swimming pool 1,240 miles (2,000 km) away in Arizona!

- Earthquakes normally last less than a minute, but they can cause a lot of damage. The sudden shake can cause **landslides**, enormous waves, and flooding. Buildings may collapse, and damage to energy supplies can cause fires.

Measuring the Shake

Earthquakes produce strong waves of energy known as **seismic waves**. Geologists measure how strong an earthquake is using an instrument called a seismograph. A weighted pen on a sensitive spring draws lines onto a roll of paper as the ground vibrates. Geologists then rate the strength of the earthquake.

Geologists rate earthquakes by the amount of energy they release. This measurement is known as **magnitude**. The **epicenter** of an earthquake is the location directly above the point where the earthquake starts underground. Geologists find the epicenter by studying the speed of the seismic waves. The **hypocenter** is the area below the surface where the earthquake began.

Think About This... ?

The Earth can be shaken up by other things, not just earthquakes. What else do you think might cause a seismograph reading?

This earthquake magintude scale shows the amount of damage to expect at each level. Each step up in magnitude means an earthquake releases 30 times more energy.

1.0 2.0 3.0 4.0 5.0 6.0 7.0 8.0 9.0 10

The Richter Magnitude Scale

BE A GEOLOGIST
Build Your Own Seismograph

You Will Need:

- a pencil
- scissors
- some paper
- a large shoebox
- a disposable cup
- a length of string
- some coins
- masking tape
- a friend to help you

adult help needed

The Geology:

The frame of a seismograph moves with the shake, but the weighted pencil stays still. With no shaking, the pencil should draw a straight line. As you shake the box, the mass of the cup and the way it is hanging means it won't move much. The paper moves and draws a squiggly line. The size of the squiggles will get bigger the harder you shake the box.

How to Make It:

Make a very long strip of paper, around 2 inches (5 cm) wide. Make two narrow slits in the sides of the shoebox, as close as possible to the bottom edge. You may want an adult to help you. The slits need to be wide enough to feed the paper strip through them.

Pierce a hole in the center of the bottom of the cup. Push the pencil through the hole, with the point facing down. Make two small holes opposite each other near the rim of the cup. Place coins around the pencil to hold it upright.

Tie some string through each hole at the rim. Poke two holes in the top of the box, the same distance apart as the cup holes. Push the string through the holes and tie the ends. Adjust the string so the tip of the pencil touches the middle of the paper strip. Now tape the base of your box to a flat surface.

Ask a friend to slowly pull the paper strip through the box. Keeping the bottom of the box in contact with the table, wobble the top of the box along the width of the paper strip. Examine your paper. Did you get a reading? Try wobbling the box in different ways and record your results.

Building for Earthquakes

When an earthquake strikes, most damage and injuries are caused by buildings collapsing. We can't stop earthquakes from happening, but understanding the geology behind earthquakes can help us design better buildings that can withstand the shaking.

standard building

Building techniques

Standard building materials can break and collapse easily during an earthquake.

quake-resistant

Earthquake-proof buildings use strong materials that absorb vibrations, and can bend and flex.

Low buildings with a large base are more earthquake-resistant than tall, narrow buildings.

low building

Known as base isolation, a building can be separated from the ground by resting it on a shock-absorbing layer. The building moves less than the shaking ground because the layer it is resting on absorbs a large part of the shock.

base isolation

HANDS-ON   Is It Safe Ground?

You will need:
- two dishes
- Jell-O
- modeling clay
- some cookies

Two buildings built exactly the same might behave differently in an earthquake. Why? The land they are built on makes a big difference. Construction companies need to check that the local geology and soil type is suitable before they start to build. This is particularly true in an earthquake zone.

Think About This...

How could you adjust your cookie building to make it more stable?

Try this simple test. Fill one dish with Jell-O and the other with modeling clay. Balance a tower of cookies on both dishes. Start to shake the dishes. Which tower falls first?

BE A GEOLOGIST
Design a Quake-Proof Building

You Will Need:

- your shake table from page 15
- marshmallows
- toothpicks
- some card stock
- tape
- scissors
- some paper clips

How to Make It:

Can you make an earthquake-resistant building using toothpicks and marshmallows?

When you have built your structure, predict how your building will behave on your shake table. Then place your building on the table and see if you were right. Make adjustments to your building and test it again.

To get a scientific result, you need to be sure your building experiences the same conditions each time you test it. Make sure you shake the table in the same direction, with the same force, and for the same length of time with each test.

Record your results. Did your adjustments improve its earthquake resistance?

Try This:

A tuned mass damper is a hanging weight that helps reduce shaking in an earthquake. How? When the building sways in one direction, the tuned mass damper moves in the opposite direction and helps keep the structure stable.

Try this simple experiment. Cut two strips of card stock. Fold the strips into a "U" shape. Then fold both ends over and tape them onto your shake table, as shown. Cut a small strip of card stock and make a small slit near the top. Slide the card stock strip onto one of the "U" shapes. Shake the table. If the damper doesn't work, add some paper clips to increase the weight. Try adding a damper to your marshmallow building. Does it work?

Underwater Earthquakes

When tectonic plates shift underwater, the resulting earthquake forces water upward, creating massive waves called **tsunamis**. Tsunamis can also be caused by underwater volcanic eruptions, underwater landslides, ice glaciers breaking off, or even a large **meteorite** hitting Earth.

When an oceanic plate is forced down into the mantle and sticks to the continental plate, it causes friction. As the sinking plate pulls the continental plate downward, it pulls it out of shape. Eventually the two plates break apart. The released stored energy as the continental plate suddenly rises pushes water upward. Powerful waves travel out in both directions.

The oceanic plate drops below the continental plate.

The plates stick, and this pulls the continental plate downward.

The plates suddenly break free, causing shock waves.

HANDS-ON Make a Tsunami Machine

You will need:
- a large plastic container
- newspaper and some mud
- water
- a piece of board
- model houses

Take a large plastic container and fill one end with scrunched-up balls of newspaper. Press mud onto the newspaper to form a sloping coastline. Place some model houses along the coast. Pour water into the other end of the container. Lay the piece of board in the water at the far end.

Quickly, and with force, lift the end of the board closest to the coastline. This action will create a large wave. What happened to your model houses? Did your tsunami harm the coast?

Tsunamis are common in the Pacific Ocean, as it has many underwater earthquakes and volcanoes. Waves can travel thousands of miles (km) across the ocean and get taller as they get closer to land. As the huge waves approach, they can cause water along the coast to be dragged out to sea for a moment. Then, a wall of water rushes onto the beach with great power. Tsunami waves can be 100 feet (30 m) high! Many communities protect their coastline by planting mangrove forests.

Think About This... ?

How do you think mangrove trees might help protect a coastline from tsunamis?

BE A GEOLOGIST
How Can We Protect Our Coasts?

You Will Need:

- a selection of plants, pebbles, and sand
- notepad and pencil

How to Do the Experiment:

Think of ways you could protect the coastline of your tsunami machine. Then test them out. Push small plants with good roots into the mud. Try placing rocks around the coastline. Make sand dunes. Predict what will happen with each experiment, and then test it out. Make sure you get accurate results by using the same amount of force when you create your tsunami.

Did any of your ideas reduce the damage?

The Geology:

Mangrove trees reduce the power of the wave. Their roots can also help form sand dunes, and catch people like a net if they get swept out to sea. Sand dunes and rocks help by acting as barriers against the waves too.

Making Mountains

Mountains are formed when tectonic plates collide, or when magma travels from the mantle up to the surface. Mountain ranges most often form along the boundaries of plates.

Types of Mountains

Mountains types get their names from how they formed.

Fold mountains form when two plates collide and Earth's crust crumples into folds. The Andes, Himalayas, and Rockies are fold mountain ranges.

Fault-block mountains form when blocks of rock at fault lines are forced up or down. The Sierra Nevada Mountains are fault-block mountains.

Volcanoes and dome mountains are both types of volcanic mountains. Volcanoes form when magma **erupts** at the surface and hardens.

Dome mountains, such as Mount St. Helens, form when magma below the surface forces the rock above to bulge.

fold mountain

fault-block mountain

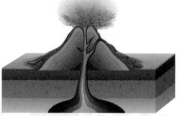

volcanic mountain

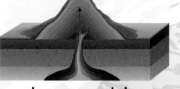

dome mountain

Think About This...

Many islands are actually the tops of underwater mountains!

BE A GEOLOGIST
Make a Fault-Block Mountain Model

You Will Need:

adult help needed

- a block of foam or a dry sponge
- some card stock
- double-sided tape
- a bread knife
- a ruler
- markers

How to Make It:

Measure the width of your sponge or foam block. Divide the width by five, and make a mark at the four points, on the top and bottom of the block. Draw a diagonal line between point 1 on the top and point 2 at the bottom. Draw a second line from point 3 at the bottom to point 4 along the top. Ask an adult to make two cuts through the sponge or foam using your lines as guides.

1   2   3   4

Trace around each cut end on some card stock. Cut the four pieces out and stick them in place on the cut edges of the sponge or foam using double-sided tape.

HANDS-ON Model Faults

Use your model to see how different mountains are made. Hold your three pieces back how they started. Push each end. The center section will rise up, forming a block mountain.

Gently pull the ends away from each other. The center will drop down again. If you continue to pull the blocks away, the center will sink, forming a **rift valley**.

scarp

horst

graben

Geologists call raised areas of fault-block mountains horsts and the sunken areas grabens. The slopes are called scarps.

Fiery Volcanoes

As Earth's tectonic plates get pulled apart, openings in the crust allow molten rock, ash, and gases to escape from the mantle. As the rock and ash cool they become solid, forming a volcanic mountain. The mountain gets bigger and bigger after each eruption.

Volcanoes are classed as either active, dormant, or **extinct**. Mount Bromo in Indonesia (pictured) is an active volcano. A dormant volcano is one that hasn't erupted for over 10,000 years.

Think About This... ❓

Fourpeaked Mountain in Alaska was thought to be extinct, but erupted in 2006. It has been renamed Fourpeaked Volcano! Do you think people should avoid calling volcanoes extinct?

Types of Volcano

The two main types of volcano are composite and shield volcanoes.

Shield volcanoes are low with shield-shaped centers and gentle slopes made by lava flows.

Composite volcanoes are steep-sided, with layers of volcanic rock made from lava, ash, and rock debris.

Under the volcano is a chamber full of molten magma.

Some volcanoes have a crater called a **caldera** that forms when a volcano collapses in on itself.

Vents take the magma to the surface.

The Pacific Ring of Fire

All around the huge Pacific plate, an area known as the Ring of Fire is home to 75 percent of the world's volcanoes and 90 percent of its earthquakes!

Pacific Ocean

HANDS-ON

Make an Erupting Volcano

You will need:

adult help needed

- a plastic bottle
- a pizza box
- some newspaper
- masking tape
- PVA glue
- some acrylic paint
- baking soda
- red food color
- hot water
- vinegar

Place the plastic bottle in the pizza box. Put scrunched up balls of newspaper around the bottle, to form a mountain shape. Stick strips of masking tape from the bottle opening down over the newspaper balls.

Tear strips of newspaper and glue them to your volcano to create a smoother surface. Then paint the volcano using acrylic paint. Add some red and orange lava flows to your brown and gray mountain.

Once your paint is dry, drop two teaspoons of baking soda into the bottle. Ask an adult to help you mix some red food color with a cup of hot water and pour it into the bottle. Then, pour in half a cup of vinegar. Your volcano should start to erupt!

Hot Spots and Ocean Vents

Most volcanic activity happens around the edge of tectonic plates, but weaknesses in the plates known as "hot spots" can cause volcanoes too. A hot spot is an area in the mantle where heat rises. Melted rock pushes through cracks in the crust to form a volcano. The volcano moves with the tectonic plate it sits on, so it cools as the plate travels away from the hot spot. Another volcano may form in the new area of plate above the hot spot. This process can produce chains of islands. A hot spot under the Pacific Plate created the volcanic islands of Hawaii in this way.

HANDS-ON
Create Hawaii!

Take a can of shaving cream and a wire rack outdoors. The shaving cream is the hot spot and the mesh is the Pacific Plate. Spray the cream upward through the rack. Then move the rack along and spray again. You will see your hot spot "islands" form along the mesh.

Hot spots under continental plates heat up groundwater under Earth's surface, causing water and steam to erupt. These eruptions are known as geysers. A geyser named "Old Faithful" in Yellowstone National Park spews water at 204 degrees F (95.6 degrees C) more than 180 feet (55 m) into the air!

Ocean Vents

Cracks in the crust under the ocean cause hot water and chemicals to escape into the ocean floor. Known as black smokers, these ocean vents eject hot, sometimes **toxic**, fluids and gas. Some sea life must like the toxic conditions, as over 590 new species have been discovered recently living near ocean vents! Giant tube worms, clams, shrimp, tiny **archaea**, and **bacteria** have all been found there.

Most of the water that comes out of black smokers is groundwater, but some of the water is from deep underground, and is coming to the surface for the very first time.

Think About This... ?

Why do you think so many new species of underwater life have been found near ocean vents?

BE A GEOLOGIST
Experiment with Magma's Density

You Will Need:

- an empty dish detergent bottle
- a large glass bowl
- some vegetable oil
- blue food color
- water
- notepad and paper
- a camera if you have one

The Geology:

Magma rises to Earth's surface for two reasons: it is forced upward by pressure, and it rises because it is less dense than the surrounding material. In this experiment, the oil is like magma in an ocean vent. It is less dense than the surrounding water so it rises to the surface.

How to Do the Experiment:

Half fill a dish detergent bottle with vegetable oil. Put on the cap and close it. Three-quarter fill the glass bowl with water. Add a couple drops of blue food color to the water and stir. Hold the bottle on its side under the water. Open the cap and gently squeeze out some oil. Draw or photograph what happens.

Magma, Lava, and Volcanic Rock

What is the difference between lava and magma? Magma is the liquid rock below the ground, inside a volcano and the Earth's mantle. When the magma reaches the surface, it is known as lava.

Magma inside this volcano has erupted. The lava flowing down the mountainside will eventually cool and form rock.

Igneous Rock

When magma cools and solidifies, it forms a type of rock known as **igneous rock**. Igneous comes from the Latin word *ignis*, which means fire. Igneous rock can be formed above or below Earth's surface. Basalt, granite, pumice, obsidian, and tuff are just some of the more than 700 types of igneous rock.

The islands of Hawaii and the oceanic plates are mostly basalt. It usually cools quickly. When it cools slowly, it forms these polygon shapes.

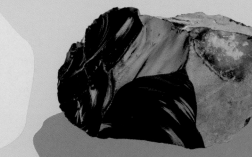

Obsidian forms as lava cools quickly above ground. It is technically not a rock, it is a volcanic glass. It can have sharp edges, so it is used to make knives and arrowheads.

Pumice forms when lava cools quickly above ground. It forms bubbles because the magma contained lots of dissolved gas. These pockets of air make the rock very light.

Dating Crust

Earth is like a giant magnet, with a North Pole and a South Pole. When new rock forms from magma, any iron in the rock orients itself with Earth's magnetic field as it cools, like a mini compass. Compasses point north, so you would expect the iron in all rock to point north too, but it doesn't. Geologists have proved that Earth's magnetic field sometimes swaps, so a compass at certain times in the past would point south, not north! Because of this, a rock's magnetic field can help geologists date how old the rock is.

It is believed the poles will swap again soon.

BE A GEOLOGIST
Examining Volcanic Rocks

You Will Need:

- a selection of rocks
- some pumice (you can find pumice at most drugstores in the nail and skincare area)
- a container
- water
- magnifying glass
- a notepad and pencil

The Geology:

Pumice forms when lava full of gas bubbles is forced out of a volcano and then cools quickly. The bubbles leave holes in the rock. The holes make pumice very light and can fill with air, causing the rock to float.

How to Do the Experiment:

Examine your collection of rocks and the pumice. Look at them through a magnifying glass. Note down what you notice about them, such as their weight and texture.

Fill a container with water. One by one, drop each rock into the water and observe what happens. Do air bubbles appear on the rocks once they enter the water? Do the rocks float or sink? How quickly do they sink? Record the results in your notepad.

If you have other volcanic rocks, such as obsidian or basalt, how do they compare to pumice. What texture are they? Do they have holes in them? Do they sink?

BASALT
Texture: very fine grains
Sink or float: sink
Density: quite heavy
Color: dark gray

PUMICE
Texture: full of holes

Glossary

archaea microorganisms which are similar to bacteria.

bacteria single-celled microorganisms that live in soil, water, the bodies of plants and animals, or matter obtained from living things.

boundary a dividing line.

caldera a large crater formed by the collapse of a volcanic cone or by an explosion.

collision a coming together with solid impact.

continental plate one of the large pieces of the surface of Earth that move separately.

continents the great divisions of land.

core the central part of Earth.

crust the outer part of Earth.

currents a body of water or air moving in a definite direction.

dense having a high mass per unit volume.

earthquakes shakings or tremblings of portions of Earth's surface.

epicenter the part of Earth's surface directly above the starting point of an earthquake.

erupts breaks through a surface.

extinct no longer active.

fault a break in Earth's crust.

fossils traces, prints, or remains of a plant or animal of a past age preserved in earth or rock.

geysers springs that now and then shoot out hot water and steam.

gravity a force of attraction between particles or bodies that occurs because of their mass.

hypocenter the point within Earth where an earthquake rupture starts.

igneous rock formed by hardening of melted earth.

landmasses continents or other large bodies of land.

landslides the slipping down of a mass of rocks or earth on a steep slope.

lava melted rock coming from a volcano.

magma molten rock material inside Earth.

magnitude the intensity of an earthquake represented by a number on a scale.

mantle the portion of Earth between the crust and the core.

meteorite a meteor, or small body of matter in the solar system, that reaches the surface of Earth.

molten melted, especially by very great heat.

oceanic plate one of the large pieces of the surface of Earth that move separately, primarily under oceans.

ridges raised or elevated parts or areas.

rift valley a long valley formed by the sinking of Earth's crust between two parallel or nearly parallel faults or groups of faults.

seismic waves elastic waves generated by an earthquake or an explosion.

sonar a device for detecting the presence and location of submerged objects by sound waves.

subduction the sideways and downward movement of the edge of a plate of Earth's crust into the mantle beneath another plate.

toxic poisonous.

trenches long, narrow, steep-sided depressions in the ocean floor.

tsunamis great sea waves produced especially by an earthquake or volcanic eruption under the sea.

volcanoes vents in Earth's crust from which melted or hot rock and steam come out.

Further Information

Museums and Places to Visit

Mountain ranges and visitors' centers. If you have a mountain range in your area, why not visit it and find out how it was formed? You may even find a dormant volcano!

Local museums will often have exhibitions and information about the area's geology. If you area is near a fault line, there may be earthquake or volcano sites you can visit!

Useful Websites

This National Geographic Kids web page has plenty of information and facts about earthquakes.
https://kids.nationalgeographic.com/explore/science/earthquake/

This great National Geographic Kids web page has information, facts, and videos all about volcanoes.
https://kids.nationalgeographic.com/explore/science/volcano/

The Geological Society's Ask a Geologist web page has loads of links about topics such as continental drift, the formation of mountains, supercontinents, and tectonic plates.
https://www.geolsoc.org.uk/Education-and-Careers/Ask-a-Geologist/Continents-Supercontinents-and-the-Earths-Crust

Books to Read

Hubbard, Ben. *Earthquakes and Tsunamis (Natural Disaster Zone)*. London, UK: Franklin Watts, 2020.

Reilly, Kathleen M. *Fault Lines & Tectonic Plates: Discover What Happens When the Earth's Crust Moves with 25 Projects*. White River Junction, VT: Nomad Press, 2017.

Publisher's note to parents and teachers: Our editors have reviewed the websites listed here to make sure they're suitable for students. However, websites may change frequently. Please note that students should always be supervised when they access the internet.

Index